MILNER CRAFT SERIES

Nerida Singleton's

DÉCOUPAGE
PROJECT KIT BOOK

With images, papers and projects

First published in 1994 by
Sally Milner Publishing Pty Ltd
558 Darling Street
Rozelle NSW 2039 Australia
© Nerida Singleton, 1994

Design by Di Quick
Photography by Bob Peters
Cover shot styling by Kathy Tripp
Pencils by Corbin and Blair, Surry Hills
Handkerchief by Linen and Lace, Balmain
Colour Separation by Litho Platemakers, SA
Printed in Australia by Impact Printing, Melbourne

National Library of Australia
Cataloguing-in-Publication data:

Singleton, Nerida, 1948-
Nerida Singleton's découpage project kit book
ISBN 1 86351 149 0.
1. Découpage. I. Title. II. Title. Découpage project kit book.
(Series: Milner craft series)
745.546

DÉCOUPAGE

The art of decorating hard surfaces using paper images is known as découpage. The original idea was to submerge cut-outs under many coats of varnish to make it look as though the image had been inlaid in the object's surface. The images are cut out, glued, varnished, sanded and waxed on surfaces that must be thoroughly prepared beforehand.

Objects

Découpage can be applied to any hard, smooth surface. Wooden boxes, trays, chairs, tables, desks, picture frames and mirrors are ideal, as are hat boxes. Plastic, porcelain, metal, glass and leather require more extensive preparation. It's best to start with a small object without hard edges, hinges and corners, such as a tablemat.

Images

Ideally, prints for découpage should be on thin paper of consistent quality and colour. Wrapping papers satisfy this requirement but they need to be sealed to prevent 'bleeding', as do pages from glossy magazines.

The best pictures are from books. Prints are also good but need to have the thickness of paper reduced. To do this, separate the corner with a fingernail, carefully pull the lifted paper to the opposite side and separate the back from the front.

Other resources include sheet music, children's picture books, art books, photographs, Japanese rice papers and postcards. Avoid papers that are extra glossy, foils, embossed papers and cards, and books and papers that are too porous. Laser colour photocopies can be used but they should be sealed several times on each side as they are particularly vulnerable to 'bleeding' and they do lose definition.

Preparation

Objects to be decorated need to be stripped of old paint or varnish, sanded, and any cracks or indentations filled and gessoed to provide a smooth surface. Gesso is a whitening plaster

compound which is mixed with glue and water and is available from art supply stores.

When applying gesso, draw it out evenly with a 2.5 cm (1 in) brush. (Liquitex gesso dries in minutes while some other varieties can take several hours to dry thoroughly.) Try to achieve an all-over coverage. Lightly sand with No 600 wet and dry sandpaper (dry) and reapply gesso by brushing in the opposite direction. You may need two or three coats depending on the depth of texture. Polish with No 0000 steel wool on completion.

It is essential to apply the sealer if you have previously applied gesso and also, it will prevent glue from penetrating a wooden surface. Towel-dry a brush or sponge applicator and use it to apply two sparing coats of Liquitex or Atelier Gloss Medium and Varnish. Apply the two coats in opposite directions. The items should be sealed both inside and out to prevent glue from seeping into the surface and affecting the adhesion of the picture.

A background can be painted with artists' acrylics, or you can use wrapping paper. Choose a colour which is sympathetic to the theme or, you might like to add contrast, or emphasise the images. When painting, apply paint evenly in one direction and when it's dry, apply another coat in the other direction. Seal when dry, as the acrylic paint is water-soluble and will smear when gluing the pictures in place.

Sealing

Papers must be sealed before cutting. Apply a sparing coat of Liquitex or Atelier Gloss Medium and Varnish to the back of wrapping papers, magazine pictures and any thick cards, calendars or photographs that have been reduced (thereby leaving a porous surface on the back). Good quality publications in book form rarely need sealer, but light body tones should be protected with sealer in case print shows through from the other side.

Seal the back of the picture first and allow to dry for 10 to 15 minutes. Then, sparingly seal the front. The picture will appear cloudy if too much sealer is applied. If you don't use all your sealed images, place them between sheets of waxed paper and file them in plastic zip folders otherwise the sealer will stick them together.

Cutting

Cut using fine-bladed, curved cuticle scissors. Never use découpage scissors for cutting anything else and cut for one hour at a time only. The curve of the blade should point away from you to allow a crisp edge on the image and you should feed the paper fluidly through the scissors, in an anti-clockwise direction if right-handed. The reverse applies to left-handed workers.

Remove any interior background first by cutting a hole in through the top, bring the scissors up from under the paper and cut in a clockwise direction. Then remove any exterior background.

Cutting finely is crucial because any remaining background will be evident under the varnish.

Design

It is essential to have a major picture which stands out as your focal point or central motif. From this you build your tonal theme, that is, you select pictures which complement the colours of the initial focal picture and you build your design around it, usually with smaller pictures which balance the original.

All pictures must be assembled before you begin gluing. Blu-Tack is indispensable when organising a preliminary layout because you can arrange and rearrange until the most appealing result is found. Organise the pictures to incorporate light, darkness and interest, and create contrasts in the work.

When laying out a design, always mark the top, bottom, back and front of an object. When working on the design for a box, the most attractive pictures should be placed on the top and the front and the less attractive ones should cover the sides, back and bottom.

Before gluing, check that none of the images will appear upside down when the object is complete. Do not cut out images before sealing and do not cut away the background until the picture is about to be used as it may be required when assembling the design. It is important to ensure that no straight lines or picture outlines are evident and this can be achieved by using pictures of flowers, leaves, tassels and jewellery to soften edges.

Gluing

Glue images one at a time to the surface using a mixture of three parts Clag (School Paste) to one part PVA - Aquadhere. Be generous with the glue as it is better to have too much rather than too little and apply to the surface of the object, placing the picture on the glued surface. Add a bit more glue to the top of the picture to allow enough emulsion to massage the image — this process eliminates excess glue and air bubbles and allows the glue to be distributed evenly behind the picture.

When an air bubble remains, you will have to cut the picture later when it is dry. Make a slit in an unobtrusive place using a small, sharp scalpel blade. Gently probe the edges and apply glue into the space. Work the glue backwards, then roll and press out. Touch up with a coloured pencil and seal.

Lightly apply a 10 cm (4 in) rubber printer's roller to the surface, radiating out from the centre and going in one direction (not backwards and forwards) with a minimum of pressure so as not to remove all the glue. Wipe glue from the roller as it builds up. Hold the work to the light to check if there is any accumulated glue or air behind the picture. When gluing is complete, remove excess using warm, clean water and a well wrung out sponge. Add a little vinegar or lemon juice if surface glue is difficult to remove. The surface should have no dull patches when observed in good light.

When dry, pencil any white edges with an appropriate oil-based colour pencil — I use mostly sepia or black — and smudge the edge if the line is too definite. This helps all the images to blend together. Sign your work with a waterproof pen or a gold fineline pen and spray lightly with fixative. When dry, seal the entire surface again with a spray fixative.

If you aren't able to finish gluing and have to leave the project overnight, clean away glue, pencil any edges, and seal the object. This prevents the pictures from losing their adhesion, especially at corners, and takes away the possibility of gremlins feasting on the glue on the pictures.

Varnishing

The many applications of varnish protect the images and, with gentle sanding between coats, it gives the effect of a flat surface — as though all the images are one sheet of paper. Always varnish in a well-ventilated, dust-free environment with good light and wear a protective mask. Work with windows open or with a fan to help get rid of fumes. Rain, damp and high humidity can create a 'bloom' (a misty effect) and you shouldn't work in sunlight.

Using a 2.5 cm (1 in) imitation sable chiselled brush (with not too long bristles), apply a coat of varnish by brushing in one direction only (not backwards and forwards). Place the brush in the middle and draw out the varnish to each side. Aim for thin coats and remember to draw the brush up against the lip of the tin to remove any excess. Use the tip of the brush to give light, quick, side-to-side sweeps across the surface to avoid air bubbles.

Allow 24 hours drying time between each coat of varnish and before reapplying, wipe surface dust particles off with a Tack Rag. Alternate directions of each coat of varnish.

Sanding

The aim of sanding is to create a uniform thickness of varnish. This can take anywhere between 30 and 100 coats and the more coats applied, the deeper the varnish and the warmer the glow. Before sanding, check that the varnished surface of the object is dry by pressing it with your finger. If an impression is left, wait another day.

After a good depth of varnish has been reached (about 20 coats), lightly sand the surface between coats. Using No 600 wet and dry sandpaper wrapped around a rubber or cork block and a few drops of water on the surface of the object, sand from side to side or up and down (in one direction). Do not use a circular motion because it will cause scratching.

Wipe off the white residue with a damp sponge, dry the object, then wipe with a Tack Rag. Colour any white edges showing on the images, seal and begin varnishing again. Repeat this sanding process from coat 20 to 28 and then change to No 1200 wet and dry sandpaper for the last three coats for final polishing.

Make sure the surface is uniformly dull. (This means there are no crevices between superimposed pictures which show tendrils of gloss.) If gloss is still evident, rub with a dry Scotchbrite, then No 0000 steel wool. Cutting compound can also be helpful at this stage. Then use the No 1200 sandpaper (wet) again to remove any scratches.

Finishes

For a full gloss surface, break down the varnish with seven parts varnish to three parts mineral turpentine. This allows an easy flow over the surface, with fewer air bubbles and brush marks.

If waxing, apply three coats (one each day) of satin or matt varnish. When it is dry, polish lightly with No 1200 wet and dry sandpaper (wet), then rub gently with No 0000 steel wool and leave for several days. For the waxed finish, put a teaspoon each of clear beeswax and Goddard's Cabinet Makers Polish in an oven or microwave and warm. (For about 20 seconds on *high* in a microwave.) Apply sparingly with a dampened cotton cloth (muslin) and work only small sections (2.5 cm or 1 in square) at a time.

Polish the surface being worked on with a soft dry cloth. Waxing should result in a hard, glass-like surface which will resist dirt. It can take from 6 to 12 months for an object to completely harden.

Materials

Découpage doesn't require a large outlay for materials — a basic kit should cost you no more than A$130. Some of these materials will be used in more than one part of the process and, depending on your project, you may need other materials like hinges for a box.

Cutting and design
Curved cuticle scissors
Blu-Tack
Cardboard template of object
Plastic zip folders and waxed paper
(for left-over pictures)

Preparation and sanding
Glass paper
Wrapping paper (optional)

Artists' acrylics and brush (optional)
No 280, 600 and 1200 wet and dry sandpaper
Cork sanding block
No 0000 steel wool
Gesso
Liquitex or Atelier Gloss Medium and Varnish
Brush for sealer and gesso
(a cheap one will do)
Scotchbrite
Beeswax stick or putty

Gluing
Clag (School Paste)
PVA-Aquadhere
Pen to sign work
(gold, fineline or waterproof)
Sponge
Towel and paper towel
Water and container
10 cm (4 in) rubber roller
Oil-based pencils (sepia, black, flesh)
Spray fixative

Varnishing and waxing
2.5 cm (1 in) imitation sable brush
Walpamur Interior/Exterior Varnish
Tack Rag
Protective mask and goggles
Mineral turpentine
Brush cleaner
Beeswax furniture polish
Goddard's Cabinet Makers Polish with Beeswax
Lint-free cotton cloth

Project 1
TABLEMAT

Using a tablemat as a first project gives you the chance to master the basic techniques of découpage while working on a flat surface without the problems of corners and edges. It means you can devote attention to cutting, assembling the design, and gluing onto a one dimensional plane. Reading the general instructions at the front of the book will help you with the process.

Method

✦ Lightly sand and remove any dust.

✦ If the tablemat has a coarse texture, apply gesso. Turn the board in clockwise revolutions to achieve an all-over coverage. Lightly sand with No 600 wet and dry sandpaper (dry) and reapply gesso by brushing in the opposite direction. You may need two or three coats depending

Step 1
Cut out the image, using good quality scissors with a sharp, curved blade

Step 2
Seal with a sparing coat of Liquitex or Atelier Gloss Medium and Varnish

on the depth of texture. Polish with No 0000 steel wool on completion.

✦ Towel-dry a brush or sponge applicator and use it to apply two sparing coats of Liquitex or Atelier Gloss Medium and Varnish which act as a sealer. Apply the two coats in opposite directions.

✦ Seal images sparingly on both sides of the paper before cutting out. Seal the back first, allow to dry for 10 to 15 minutes, then, seal the front.

✦ Cut the images precisely, eliminating the unrequired interior areas before cutting the outline and removing all white background from the edges.

✦ Choose your focal picture and arrange the pictures on a template to attain the overall effect of the design.

✦ If you wish to paint a background, use artists' acrylics. Apply paint evenly in one direction. When dry, apply another coat in the other direction. Seal when dry, as the acrylic paint is water-soluble and will smear when gluing the pictures in place.

Covering the mat with wrapping paper is another background option. When applying wrapping paper, first seal it on both sides with spray fixative or sealer. Press the edges of the wrap over the edges of the tablemat, turn the paper over and there will be definite impression lines. It is important to remember that the paper must be sealed before any cutting is done. Cut the wrapping paper slightly larger than the lines to allow for errors. Because the paper is already sealed it is less likely to stretch when the glue is rolled out.

Place a generous amount of glue onto the mat and spread it over the surface with your fingers, being careful to spread the glue along all edges and corners. Position the wrapping paper on the mat and add more glue on top. Massage the

Step 3
Start by gluing down the
focal picture

Step 4
Roll out the picture, using
long strokes

glue with the finger-tips, then, working quickly and using a roller with very gentle pressure, start rolling out the glue from under the paper.

✦ Glue down the focal picture. Glue each image separately and be sure each is secure and has no air bubbles or excess glue underneath before proceeding to the next picture.

✦ Using a roller and very light pressure, roll out the picture by using long strokes, radiating them outwards from

the centre of the image. Continue gluing images in this manner.

✦ When gluing is complete, remove excess using warm, clean water and a well wrung out sponge.

✦ When dry, pencil any white edges and smudge them slightly if the colour is too obvious a contrast with the images. Sign your work with a water-proof pen or a gold fineline pen and spray lightly with fixative. When dry, seal the entire surface again.

Step 5
Apply a coat of varnish, brushing in one direction only

Step 6
Sanding with No 600 wet and dry sandpaper (after 20 coats of varnish)

◆ Apply a coat of varnish, brushing in one direction only. Place the loaded brush in the centre of the mat and draw the varnish out to each side with light, quick, side-to-side sweeps across the surface to avoid air bubbles. Aim for thin coats.

◆ Allow to dry in a well-ventilated, dust-free environment. Apply only one coat each day. Wipe the surface with a Tack Rag to remove any accumulated dust particles, then varnish again in the opposite direction. Apply 20 coats of varnish before sanding.

◆ Sand with No 600 wet and dry sandpaper after each coat until you reach 28 coats. Change to No 1200 and polish after each coat to 30 coats.

◆ Give a final coat of gloss varnish, being aware of air bubbles, surface dust, and brush strokes which might spoil your surface.

◆ If waxing the tablemat, give three coats (one each day) of satin or matt varnish. Rub gently with No 0000 steel wool. Apply beeswax and buff to a gentle sheen.

Step 7
Rub gently with No 0000 steel wool after a coat of satin or matt varnish

Step 8
Completed tablemat, and some of the stages involved

Project 2

BOX

lways keep the focus of the design on the top and front of the box with less emphasis on the bottom and sides. The background can be painted, covered with wrapping paper, or created from pictures. Reading the general instructions at the front of the book will help you with the process.

Method

◆ Mark the top and bottom of one side of the box (inside) to make sure it will fit flush when hinged. Check for crevices which may need to be filled with beeswax stick or putty. Beeswax is preferable because it doesn't shrink. If using filler, apply with a spatula and be generous with the filler because it shrinks as it dries.

◆ Sand the box well with glass paper, then lightly with No 280 wet and dry sandpaper and wipe clean.

◆ If the box has a coarse texture, apply gesso — drawing it out evenly — with a 2.5 cm (1 in) brush. Try to achieve an all-over coverage. Lightly sand with No 600 wet and dry sandpaper (dry) and reapply gesso by brushing in the opposite direction. You may need two or three coats

depending on the depth of texture. Polish with No 0000 steel wool on completion.

◆ Seal images sparingly on both sides of the paper before cutting. Seal the back first, allow to dry for 10 to 15 minutes, then, seal the front.

◆ Cut the images precisely, eliminating the unrequired interior areas before cutting the outline and removing all white background from the edges.

- Cut a cardboard template for each surface and, using Blu-Tack, arrange and rearrange your design. Begin with your focal picture and build up complementary images until you are satisfied with the effect.

- Pictures which cover a corner and travel down the sides will have to be mitred at the corners.

- If desired, paint the background with artists' acrylics at least twice, applying each coat in different directions.

- Seal the box with acrylic Liquitex Gloss Medium and Varnish, drawing the sealer out well so no bumps and lumps are evident. Seal the inside and rims of the box.

- Using a mixture of three parts Clag (School Paste) to one part PVA-Aquadhere, apply a generous amount of glue to the surface and smear with fingertips until silky. Make sure there are no areas that have no glue, or have lumps of hard glue, before putting the pictures down. Massage a little extra glue on top of the picture until the glue becomes tacky and the picture and the surface start to bond. The glue needs to be distributed evenly behind each picture.

- Add a little more glue and, using a 5 cm (2 in) or 10 cm (4 in) rubber roller, roll with very gentle pressure from the centre of the picture and radiate out to the edges. Hold work to the light to check if there is any accumulated glue or air behind the picture. Wipe the glue from the roller as it builds up.

- Using a damp sponge, wipe the excess glue from the surface of your picture.

- Allow to dry, then check each image for white edges. Colour with an appropriate oil-based colour pencil and smudge edge if the line is too definite.

- Sign and date your work with a waterproof pen. If using a gold fineline pen, spray

COMPLETED JEWELLERY BOX, AND SOME OF THE STAGES INVOLVED

sparingly with workable fixative when ink is dry, otherwise it will smear under sealer. Allow fixative to dry.

◆ Sparingly seal all surfaces.

◆ Always use your protective mask and make sure you have good ventilation when varnishing. Use a fine imitation sable brush, beginning at the top and using light sweeps in one direction. Be sure to brush out any accumulation of varnish which builds up where the top and sides of the box join. Check for drips and don't allow a thick build-up at rims.

◆ Place both sections of the box on tins to allow the air to circulate and dry them. Allow 24 hours drying time between each coat of varnish and, before reapplying, wipe surface dust particles off with a Tack Rag. Alternate directions of each coat of varnish.

◆ When 20 coats have been applied, begin sanding lightly with No 600 wet and dry sandpaper (wet) in one direction, with sandpaper wrapped around a rubber or cork block. Wipe off the white residue with a damp sponge, dry, then colour any white edges showing on the images, seal and begin varnishing again.

◆ Repeat the sanding process using No 600 wet and dry sandpaper until the surface is quite flat. (This may take somewhere between 30 and 50 coats of varnish.)

After each of the last three coats of varnish, use No 1200 sandpaper for the final polishing. Remove the build-up of varnish at the rims of the box using a scalpel or paring knife.

◆ Make sure the surface is uniformly dull. If gloss is still evident, rub with a dry Scotchbrite, then No 0000 steel wool. Cutting compound can also be helpful at this stage.

- If you want a gloss finish, apply a light coat of varnish broken down seven parts varnish to three parts mineral turpentine. Make sure there are no air bubbles in the surface and place the box in a dust-free environment to dry. Repeat this process until the surface is perfectly smooth.

- For a waxed finish, put a teaspoon each of clear beeswax and Goddard's Cabinet Makers Polish in an oven or microwave and warm. (For about 20 seconds on *high* in a microwave). Apply sparingly with a dampened cotton cloth (muslin) and work only small sections at a time. Repeat if necessary. Apply a final coat of Goddard's over the entire surface and repeat often during the curing time to enhance the box. It can take from 6 to 12 months for an object to completely harden.

- Use a 2 mm (5/64 in) drill bit for all the fittings and start with the corners. Always use fittings with screws rather than those secured by nails. Using an electric drill and a 2 mm (5/64 in) bit, secure brass corners. Next work on the handle and then the top. It is easier to manipulate the fittings before the hinges have been attached.

- To attach the hinges, measure an equal distance from the ends and drill opposite sides in sequence. Add the clasp last and choose one that has a padlock. It is best to secure the top of the clasp and then line up the underneath section to ensure that it is not too loose. An antique padlock and handles can give the box a great deal of style.

- Paint the inside of the box rims with artists' acrylics. Allow to dry. Apply 2 coats of sealer, allowing time to dry between each coat.

SOME OF THE MANY SOURCES OF IMAGES TO USE FOR DECOUPAGE

I'm simply too tired to Write.

A Happy Christmas

There's magic in her voice,
There's witchcraft in her eye,
But her lips when pressed together,
Ope the gates of Paradise.

Best Wishes

Wishing you
a joyful
Christmas.

Printed in Germany.

EUROPE ASIA

AFRICA

AUSTRALIA

N. AMERICA

S. AMERICA

FROM THE
DEAR HOMELAND.

Should
Old
Acquaintance
be Forgot.

WISHES
TRUE

MRS. BOW AND ALL THE LITTLE WOWS.

MRS. GOAT AND HER TWO KIDS.

NEW YEAR
WISHES.

Add Joy, add Health,
then Bliss, then Wealth,
Then Happiness and
✤ ✤ ✤ Pleasure,
Then add to these ✤
✤ a life of ease,
Again add Love ✤
✤ and Treasure,
Divide away pain
✤ and decay,
Let griefs subtracted be,
Long life supply;
✤ then multiply
The "Whole" I wish for thee.

LUCAS CLASSEY.

BEAGLES' POSTCARDS

I am the light of the world.
John 8:12.

GOOD LUCK

Merry Christmas

A Christmas Greeting

To Greet You.

That you'll re - mem - ber me

Love's Symbols

Do pop in for tea,
you are always
welcome any day
at 4 o'clock.
AKA

Rococo

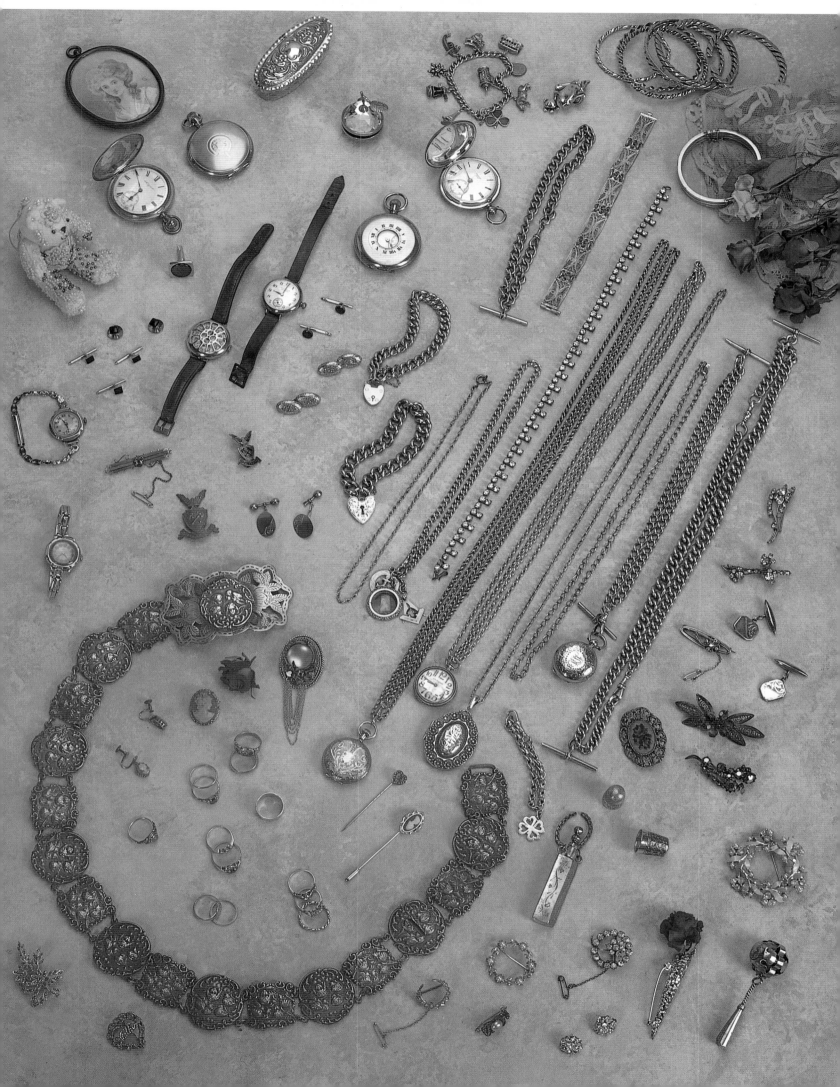